*Hello and welcome to my first ever book. My name is Rob Parsor
a Camera'. Why are you called that? I hear you ask. Well, it's a simple explanation. Whenever I'm out walking I always have a large camera dangling around my neck and people often ask if I am a professional photographer, to which my answer has always been 'no, I'm just a walker with a camera'.*

I was born in 1971 in the village of Stock, Essex. A great deal of my childhood found me outdoors playing football, going fishing or cycling around the local woods. I inherited my love of the great outdoors from my parents and spent many happy days walking with my Mum during the school holidays. My 7th birthday found me in possession of my first camera and this came with me on our walks, snapping anything and everything. I met my wife, Jean, in 1992 and most weekends we were off exploring the coast and countryside of Essex, Suffolk and Kent before moving to Cornwall in 1998. We loved the Cornish coastline and photographing the magnificent sunsets from the coast around the Tintagel area became the usual evening routine. I was also drawn to the wild open spaces of Dartmoor and often found myself venturing across the border into Devon to spend time in this wonderful landscape, exploring and photographing every last inch of the moor. 2001 saw our first holiday to the Lake District and we instantly fell in love with the land of lakes and mountains. Holidays to the Lakes became ever more frequent, with Wainwright 'bagging' becoming the latest hobby. We realised that resistance was futile, relocating to Cumbria in 2017.

I was lucky to find work close to home and my commute consists of a cycle ride through the beautiful Eden Valley with plenty of landscape and wildlife photographic opportunities en-route. Spare time usually finds us exploring the amazing countryside with plenty of time to walk in my beloved fells. As mentioned earlier I do not regard myself as a professional and only shoot in jpeg, preferring to spend my time walking to sitting in front of a laptop editing the hundreds of photos which I take. Therefore the photographs contained in this book may not be technically brilliant; however I do hope they go some way to conveying the drama and beauty of the Lake District in winter.
Enjoy the views,
Rob.

Please follow Just a Walker with a Camera
on Facebook, Instragram & Twitter

Little Book Company.org
from The Calendar Company

A beautiful January day on the fells around Glencoyne. I spotted the small rock in the foreground and loved the way it mimicked the shapely peak of Catstycam, which I always think looks like a 'proper mountain looking mountain'. With steep sloping sides and pointed summit it proudly takes its place as a guardian of the Helvellyn range, connected to its more illustrious neighbour via the dragon backed ridge of Swirral Edge, which makes for an exciting day out in the mountains when combined with the opposing ridge of Striding Edge. When the crowds are swarming the summit of Helvellyn, head to Catstycam as it is likely you will find peace and solitude.

The Coniston Range from Fairfield

Looking back whilst climbing Fairfield from Grisedale Tarn, I noticed that the Coniston range had started to appear through the low shifting clouds. A late afternoon sun added a pink hue to the sky, enhancing an already delightful scene. The Old Man of Coniston towers above the village of Coniston, staring down like a protective parent. His view would have been temporarily obscured on this day though, as clouds swirled around his head. Every year, thousands of walkers climb to the summit but he is just part of a truly magnificent range of fells, all of which deserve their own exploration.

5

Brothers Water Reflections

On a calm day it's difficult to find a more beautiful location than Brothers Water. Here, a dusting of snow enhances the majesty of the surrounding fells, with Hartsop Dodd taking centre stage. A pleasant couple of hours can easily be spent strolling around the circular route that encompasses the water and it would be rude not to call in for a pint at the Brothers Water Inn, which enjoys a stunning view up to Dove Crag.

The slopes of Silver How, above Grasmere, having been transformed into a magical winter wonderland by a fresh fall of snow. The cloud formations lend depth to the scene while the two walkers give it a sense of scale. Silver How is an unassuming fell which forms a picturesque backdrop to the waters of Grasmere. A good choice of routes wind their way up the relatively gentle slopes to the summit which enjoys lovely views down into the surrounding valleys, with the scene across Grasmere to Loughrigg being a particular favourite of mine.

9

It's a Hard Life

The residents of the high fells have a tough life when the snows arrive. However, they have ably adapted to their surroundings and will dig through the snow to reach the succulent grasses and foliage below. Usually you will encounter Herdwick sheep on the high fells, however this is a Swaledale. Named after the Yorkshire valley of Swaledale, they are well suited to the mountainous regions of the UK being extremely hardy with thick coarse coats. The ewes make excellent, well attentive mothers and are renowned for being able to rear lambs in adverse weather conditions.

11

Striding Edge, connecting Birkhouse Moor to Helvellyn, is arguably the most iconic location in the Lake District, calling to thousands of people every year to come and test themselves on its airy delights. A route just below the jagged arête provides walkers an alternative to the spine tingling traverse along the very top but both routes require some scrambling and in full winter conditions it becomes the domain of experienced walkers and climbers only.

13

Blencathra from Eamont Bridge

A gorgeous winter sunset from the small village of Eamont Bridge with the instantly recognisable silhouette of Blencathra, clearly showing why it has the alternative name of Saddleback. Eamont Bridge can be found just to the south of Penrith, on the North Eastern edge of the Lake District, and is home to the Neolithic henges of King Arthur's Round Table and Mayburgh, with the latter being particularly impressive whilst enjoying commanding views to the Pennines and the fells of Lakeland.

15

A Frozen Lake Windermere

A December day which had seen a huge snowfall overnight meant that it was impossible to drive anywhere. So it was a pleasant surprise to discover that the ferry was still running across Lake Windermere, by cutting its way through the ice. Crossing to the Western shore whilst heeding the words of warning "don't be long as I don't know how long the ferry will be running for", a quick walk was rewarded by the unusual scene of the boats on the lake surrounded by ice and snow.

Following the wall up Fairfield from Hause Gap during a stunning December day. The wall and clouds combine to add depth to the shot and, again, two walkers obligingly add to the sense of scale. Fairfield itself forms the centre piece of the much loved classic Lakeland round known as the Fairfield horseshoe, which is a classic high level ridge route starting from either Ambleside or Rydal. Fantastic views unfold throughout the route with the magnificent vista from the north edge of Fairfield, across the Grisedale valley to Helvellyn, being particularly memorable.

19

The Arctic Tundra?

It's always difficult to convey the atmosphere of a particular day in a still image but I think this one does the trick. Up on Nethermost Pike, during a bitterly cold November day, the wind was screaming across the mountain tops whipping the surface snow into swirling spindrift demons which spiralled their way across the fells, momentarily obscuring the fabulous views and turning the landscape into a bleak arctic tundra like scene.

One of the most magical days I've ever spent in the fells with an overnight heavy snowfall coating the landscape. Fresh, deep, virgin snow is gorgeous to look at but incredibly difficult to walk through if you are the first person up in the morning. However, the effort is totally worth it when you are confronted with views such as this. The grass tussocks around Angle Tarn had been transformed into snow domes and a thin layer of ice had formed around the tarn edges. A slight breeze was disturbing the water surface with a low viewpoint managing to capture the reflection of Angletarn Pikes.

23

Winter Sunlight on Scales Fell, Blencathra

Blencathra always proves popular when the snow arrives, as it's easily accessible from the A66. The low winter sun, filtering through cloud, often creates lovely soft lighting up in the mountains and it's always worth taking several shots in close succession as the scene is constantly changing. This photo was taken late in the day, looking back up from Scales Fell. I liked the stream of people making their way down after enjoying an unforgettable day.

25

Riggindale Beck in Full Flow

If weather is proving unsuitable for landscape photography then it is always worth seeking out the becks and streams which snake their way down from the fells. Winter usually finds them full with rain or meltwater and the small cascades make for beautiful sights. This photo was taken on a walk around Haweswater on a cloudy, extremely windy, February day and I just managed to coincide it with a fleeting sunny moment.

For me, the Langdale Pikes are a perfectly formed slab of mountain architecture with Pike o' Stickle standing proud, as viewed here from Pike o' Blisco. Pike o' Stickle is home to several Neolithic Stone Age axe factories, which can be found above the scree slopes on the severely steep southern face of the fell. Also in this photo can be seen the distant bulk of Skiddaw which has a stream of cloud tracking across the summit, making it appear as a smouldering volcano.

I am lucky that my work commute involves a cycle through the grounds of the Lowther Estate. This does mean that sometimes I have to apologise for being slightly late due to photographing the resident red squirrels, deer and hares or a scene such as this, with a low January sun illuminating a light mist hovering above the dew laden grass beyond the fence.

31

Frozen Cairn on Nethermost Pike

An incredibly cold day on the Helvellyn range, with a ferocious wind dropping the temperature to around -20°c. This cairn on Nethermost Pike had been coated in rime ice, which forms when supercooled water droplets freeze onto cold surfaces. Days like these, where nature reminds you who is boss, are the ones which live longest in the memory as you pitch yourself against weather that most people will never experience in their lifetime. The huge bulk of St Sunday Crag can be seen in the middle distance and provides a perfect backdrop to the cairn.

Frozen Swan Lake

A cold, misty, deserted Grasmere resulted in slim pickings for the resident swans, who were wading around in what appeared to be a giant 'slush puppie'. Grasmere village and the adjacent lake are popular tourist destinations and have associations with the Lakes poets, especially William Wordsworth who lived in the village for many years. Despite it being a tourist hotspot I always enjoy a visit to the area with many fine walks radiating from the village, although it is extremely rare to find no one around on the lake shore and the swans are usually well catered for.

Misty morning at Elterwater

An early morning November sun just managing to penetrate the mist on the lane from the village of Elterwater to the quarry, before I embarked on a climb of Lingmoor Fell. Elterwater is a delightful small village deriving its name from nearby Elter Water, where a beautifully scenic, easy walk can be enjoyed along the river Brathay to Skelwith Bridge. Misty, sunny mornings always make for memorable walking with plenty of opportunities for atmospheric photos, especially if trees can be included in the scene.

Snow Sparkles

On a crystal clear winters day, with the sun beating down on freshly fallen snow, the landscape can appear as though thousands of diamonds have been scattered across the surface (it hasn't, I've checked!). This phenomenon occurs when the sun reflects off flat snowflakes on the surface. Each sparkle is a reflection of the sun from single crystals, as seen here on the slopes between High Hartsop Dodd & Little Hart Crag.

39

Gratefully following a trail laid down by an earlier pioneer, through the deep snow to Blease Fell. The previous day had witnessed heavy snowfall, resulting in cornices forming along the edges of the summit. This shot shows the potential danger of venturing too close to the edge and the footprints did skirt a little too close for comfort at times. Once again, thank you to whoever you are for bringing a sense of scale to proceedings.

41

The Crags of Nethermost Pike

A slight dusting of November snow had fallen overnight on the higher fells, so I ventured up onto the Helvellyn range. I wasn't prepared for quite how windy it was on the top with gusts rampaging across the fells, knocking me off my feet on three occasions. Somehow I managed to keep the camera steady enough to take this shot of Nethermost Pike, with the snow etching out the crags making it appear as a real life Wainwright drawing.

43

Grasmere Reflections

After spending a glorious day exploring the fells above the village, I descended to the lake shore to be greeted by this beautiful sight of the surrounding snow plastered fells reflected in the glassy stillness of Grasmere. I then made my way back to the village where it is almost obligatory to pay a visit to Sarah Nelson's gingerbread shop, if for no other reason than to stand outside, sniff the air and inhale the sweet spicy aroma of freshly baked gingerbread.

45

On Sharp Edge

Sharp Edge is arguably the most exciting route up onto Blencathra (Hall's Fell could also justifiably lay claim to this title) and a good head for heights is required. As with Striding Edge only the most experienced walkers will venture here in full winter conditions. This shot was taken during a late cold snap in April with the patches of powdery snow, lying in the crevices, actually providing extra grip for the ascent. It was a beautiful calm, clear day and the view down to Scales Tarn was exceptional.

A low January sun illuminating the glassy surface of Ullswater, from the slopes of Place Fell. One of the Ullswater steamers can be seen creating ripples, whilst ploughing its way back towards Glenridding. Place Fell is a beautiful mountain to explore with a whole day easily spent walking between the separate fell tops that make up its enormous bulk. An early morning winter climb can be rewarded not only with the low sun lighting up this glorious view but can also provide encounters with the resident herd of red deer that roam the slopes. Be warned though that they will spot you long before you see them, so a fair amount of stealth is required.

Sometimes You Just Have to Stop and Stare

A lone walker stopping for a moment on Dove Crag to take in the stunning vista of the Coniston range. Sometimes it's easy to forget to just stop and take in the scenery around you. I always try to spend at least fifteen minutes on summits, to simply stare at the views and commit them to memory for revisiting on the days that I can't be out on the fells.

The View from High Hartsop Dodd

An incredibly tough morning, trail breaking up the face of High Hartsop Dodd. The snow was 3' deep in places, making it extremely slow going. Stopping to catch my breath (also known as stopping to admire the view) on the way up I looked back to see the twin peaks of Angletarn Pikes reflecting in the mirror like surface of Brothers Water. I particularly liked the way that the ruined wall followed the undulating skyline.

53

Dwarfed by Grasmoor

A simple photo of the mighty face of Grasmoor from Buttermere. Although it is a simple shot I really like it as it reminds me of a scene from Lord of the Rings with the walkers on the ridge being dwarfed (or hobbited if you prefer?) by the huge bulk of the mountain. The walkers would have been heading back to Buttermere, which is one of my favourite villages in the Lake District and an infinitely more pleasant destination than Mordor.

55

A Frosty Helvellyn Summit

Looking down on the cross walled shelter from the frosty, cloud bound summit of Helvellyn. The shelter was designed this way so it could provide protection from the wind, whatever the direction. Unfortunately on this occasion the wind was coming from all directions, howling like a banshee across the neighbouring fells and swirling like a skyborne maelstrom around the summit, rendering the shelter redundant and, more importantly, meant that I had to postpone my planned coffee break.

57

Snow Clad Langdale Pikes

As mentioned previously the Langdale Pikes are a truly magnificent sight, especially when dressed in their winter clothing. The twin peaks of Loft Crag and Harrison Stickle stand like imperious guardians of the Langdale valley, starkly contrasting with the spring like conditions below. They just seem to know how gorgeous they look and make no pretence of hiding their smugness. This is one of the magnificent views that can be enjoyed on the easy walk between the villages of Elterwater and Skelwith Bridge, as described earlier in this book.

Blizzard in Pooley Bridge

A February day, merrily minding my own business photographing the resident red squirrels and deer of Dunmallard Hill, when out of nowhere a snow blizzard swept in and turned the landscape from green and brown to black and white within thirty minutes. It certainly made for an entertaining afternoon of walking with the coffee and cake interlude at Granny Dowbekins café even more welcome than usual, even if the drive back home was a little 'interesting'.

61

During February my cycle to work becomes interesting once again, with the landscape starting to materialise from the eternal darkness of the winter mornings. The resident wildlife start to emerge tentatively from the surrounding woodland, staring inquisitively as I pass on by. Sunrise eventually coincides with my journey and occasionally I am treated to sights such as this, leaving me to explain why I'm late for work...again.

63

Many people will summit Dove Crag as part of the classic Fairfield horseshoe, following the partly ruined wall down the slope to the next summit of High Pike. This walker was doing just that whilst keeping a distance from the wall as the snow had drifted up against the east side, making the going somewhat arduous.

On a calm day, Elter Water provides a stunning canvas for reflections of the distant Langdale Pikes. On this January day, however, a slight breeze was disturbing the surface and photographic opportunities looked bleak. I was about to give up when the sun popped out, lighting up the reed bed as a swan cruised into view and completed the shot.

The most jaw-droppingly, beautiful day I have ever been out walking in with fresh virgin snow plastering the landscape, transforming it into an Arctic like location. The snow was waist deep in places making it hard going to reach the twin summits of Angletarn Pikes but completely worth the effort for this view across the tarn to Brock Crags. I spent the rest of the day circumnavigating Angle Tarn via Brock Crags and just generally staring at the beauty that surrounded me.

An early morning climb of Catbells to capture a sunrise which unfortunately never emerged from behind a stubborn cloud bank. Thankfully, later on the cloud started to part and lift, revealing a view to the distant bulk of Blencathra which was enhanced by the sunlight dancing across its slopes contrasting nicely with the dark foreboding sky. Catbells is an immensely popular fell often described as 'family friendly', although it is slightly more difficult than people realise with a little section of scrambling required on the usual route up from Hawse End. It is a little gem of a fell, shining like a diamond within the jewels of the Newlands valley with fabulous views over Derwent water to the mighty giants of Skiddaw & Blencathra being especially memorable.

A Sunbathed Glenridding

An early January morning on Glenridding Dodd. After a climb from the National Trust car park at Glencoyne bay, the sun poked through the clouds creating a beautiful scene. The village of Glenridding bathed in a soft light while colours danced and swirled through the mist hanging over Ullswater. Glenridding Dodd is a modest little fell, which is really just the termination of its neighbour, Sheffield Pike. However, it does have an interesting summit with small pools and rocky outcrops to explore and is great for a quick morning or evening 'view fix'.

73

Stybarrow Dodd from Sheffield Pike

Sunlit cloud spilling over the snow topped Stybarrow Dodd, with the dark skies beyond creating a contrasting dramatic backdrop. Sheffield Pike enjoys a commanding position between the glens of Glencoyne and Glenridding , with the view across to the Helvellyn range being particularly sublime (as seen previously in this book). The route over Green Side and up onto Stybarrow Dodd is a relatively easy, peaceful alternative to the usual paths up to Helvellyn.

75

Splintered rocks stand like grey sentinels, defiant against the elements on Loadpot Hill. While Loadpot itself will never top the list of anyone's favourite fells, with it forming the northern terminus of the High Street range with an uninspiring summit, it does command a lovely view across to the Helvellyn range. Most walkers will pass by quickly, pausing momentarily at the trig point before re-joining the ancient roman road, which gives High Street its name. One item of interest on the way is a pile of rocks which is all that remains of the chimney of Lowther House, an old shooting lodge, located not far south of the summit.

77

Winter Droving

The Winter Droving is a rural celebration which honours the herding of animals from long distances to the market town of Penrith. Event highlights include live music, street entertainers, market stalls and the culmination of festivities end with a masked lantern procession through the town. In 2018 the winter droving also came to the village of Pooley Bridge from where this photo was taken.

This is the kind of view that I live for. Shafts of dancing light, from a low winter sun, penetrate through broken cloud to illuminate Dollywaggon Pike. The crags and crevices have been accentuated by a dusting of snow – it really doesn't get much better than this! I spotted the ravens circling around and waited for them to pass by in front of the Pike, completing the shot.

When the snow line is high up on the fells, it almost feels as though you are entering a different world when you climb from a sun drenched green valley up into the monochromic world of the snow topped mountains. The effort is paid out in full when looking back to a sight such as this from Crinkle Crags. The bottom of the beautiful Langdale valley is illuminated by an afternoon sun, casting shadows along the flanks of the surrounding fells which then blend into the well-defined snow line.

83

All Calm on Ullswater

On a beautiful calm February afternoon a steamer plies its trade along Ullswater, between the lakeshore villages of Glenridding and Pooley Bridge. The majestic, snow etched, Helvellyn range provides the backdrop to an already enchanting scene. Ullswater is often described as the most beautiful stretch of water in the Lake District and on days like this it's hard to disagree. Following the devastation that storm Desmond wreaked upon the area, a new walking trail was created encircling Ullswater with the intention of enticing people back to the villages around its shores. The Ullswater Way is 20 miles of pure walking delight which can be tackled in one unforgettable day trek or by breaking the trail into more manageable chunks and utilising the Ullswater steamers to travel between the start and finish points.

Frosted Grasses

Sometimes you need to tear your eyes away from the views and focus on the details of your immediate surroundings, as Mother Nature casts her weird and wonderful spells on the world around you. I really liked the look of these snow frosted grasses on the slopes of Whitestones with the Helvellyn range providing a picturesque backdrop.

87

Frosted rocks on Scafell

A bitterly cold, snow free January afternoon on Scafell with a view down to Wastwater. It could almost be a summer's day with only the frost covered foreground rocks providing a clue to the temperature. I loved the way that the low sun was casting horizontal shadows along the flanks of Yewbarrow. Scafell often gets overlooked in favour of its more illustrious neighbour but the difficulty of traversing from Scafell Pike means that you will often have the gorgeous views all to yourself while the hordes jostle for selfie position on England's highest point.

"Do the Shake, the Sheepy Sheepy Shake"

A sudden blizzard on the shores of Thirlmere and this Herdwick is not impressed with her new snow covered coat and takes time out of her busy grass cutting schedule to shake it off. Herdwick sheep are native to the Lake District and are renowned for their hardiness and ability to live high up in the fells. The lambs graze with their mothers on the 'heaf' (sheep pasture) belonging to the farm, instilling a life long knowledge of their grazing area. I regard the Herdwicks as guardians of Lakeland as they are responsible for maintaining the look of the landscape which I love.

Following the Fusedale beck from Howtown is a delightful route up onto the High Street range via Wether Hill. The valley is a beautiful location whatever the season but with snow enhancing the contours of the surrounding fells it becomes truly magical. You won't meet many other people and the only sound you will hear is the trickling of the beck, as it lazily meanders its way down towards Ullswater. A quiet approach may reward you with a sighting of the resident red deer, which is always a pleasure.

Sunlight illuminating the edges of Doddick Fell & Scales Fell on Blencathra. Yet again I'm indebted to a couple of walkers who help to emphasise the vastness of this landscape. Snow really helps to show off mountain landscapes with the whiteness contrasting with the shadows adding real depth to the scenes.

Temperature inversion, cloud inversion, radiation fog: call it what you like (someone more intelligent than myself can explain the differences, professor Google will be able to help) all are amazing sights to behold, with the world below obscured from view and surrounding peaks appearing like Himalayan giants poking their heads through the clouds.

Frozen Tarn on Loadpot Hill

When wandering up in the fells I always like to seek out the small tarns and bodies of water, as they provide an interesting focal point for photographs. Usually they act as reflective pools for the sky but not on this occasion. Instead the solidly frozen tarn provided a beautiful foreground to the stunning array of fells beyond.

And finally, a rare photo of myself doing what I love best, standing on a mountain top and staring at the view. This was taken on Slight Side just after I had climbed my 214th and final summit of my first round of the Wainwright fells.

I hope you have enjoyed the views in this book and they have either brought back memories of your own adventures or have inspired you to get out in the fells and explore them for yourself. Please remember that mountains can be dangerous places in these conditions, so pay a visit to the BMC (British Mountaineering Council) website for advice on winter walking.

Published and printed in the UK by Little Book Company,
part of The Calendar Printing Company Ltd.